Contents

Quicksilver Country Dances **4**

   English Country Dancing and the I 4

   Some Technical Bits 5

   Glossary of Dance Figures 6

   The Steps 8

Quick & Easy Dances **9**

   1. Circassian Circle 9

   2. Sandridge Reel 10

   3. Mixer Promenade 11

   4. Jumping Johnny 12

   5. Oxo Reel 13

   7. Tars of Victory 15

Quite Simple Dances **16**

   8. Hop Pickers Picnic 16

   9. Mr Cosgill's Delight 17

   10. The Haystack 18

   11. Barley Water 19

Rather Older Dances **20**

   12. Clog Brawle 20

   13. Washerwoman's Brawle 21

   14. Sellingers Round 22

   15. Farandole 23

   Mike Ruff 25

   Quicksilver 25

   Other Publications by Mike Ruff 26

Quicksilver Country Dances

The Maypole Madness CD from Quicksilver was recorded to provide music for The Maypole Manual. This is the bands version of the CD and it was designed for dancing and so here are some dances for you to try that do not need a Maypole. There are 7 really easy dances suitable for young children, inexperienced dancers (or teachers) or just very short lessons. After that there are 4 which introduce some new moves, steps & styles. Finally there are 3 tracks for Tudor Dances which are simple enough to include and a track of tunes from that period which works for a medieval dance so there is a bit of instant history

Some of the dances are well known traditional ones that you might find at any English barn dance or ceilidh or are simple adaptions of them. In a few cases I have taken a more obscure & complex dance from history and re-written it to make it a little simpler or to fit the music. This process is quite common and has always been happening. I have taken some liberties (but not too many) and would definitely encourage you to do the same.

The track numbers given are for the Maypole Madness CD. If you are using the Maypole Manual CD the tracks may be slightly different, please see the table on page 24.

English Country Dancing and the Music

English Country Dancing as we know it has been in existence for nearly 500 years. It has been danced by all levels of society and was the dominant dance style during much of the 17th & 18th centuries. As with any other art form it has changed and evolved, being influenced by what people were wearing, where they did their dancing and the music of that was being played at the time. These changes are still going on and it remains a thriving, living tradition danced by people of all ages and in many different places.

The music that is played for country dancing has been equally varied, often influenced by what by instruments were available at any time. Anything from pipe and tabor to fiddles, a piano or an accordion could be used as well as full bands, orchestras and, of course, recorded versions of all the above for much of the last 100 years. The tunes that are played are equally varied and it is often up to the musicians so you can find classical, pop, jazz & swing featuring amongst much older tunes.

Some Technical Bits

Country Dancing is almost always danced by couples and that used always to mean a boy dancing with a girl and the dances were described that way. Nowadays it rarely matters who dances with who but they sometimes do different things so you might need to have 1s & 2s.

Then it is all about the dancers making patterns called figures. So with quite a small number of figures you can have lots of dances which is what I have done here. Each figure will fit to a phrase of music or half a phrase. A phrase is usually 8 bars (or 16 steps) so half a phrase is 4 bars. Many tunes are 32 bars or 4 phrases long (two sections repeated AABB) so you only have 4 figures to learn

The main rhythms used are the polka and the reel in 2/4 & 4/4 and the jig in 6/8. There are also hornpipes and waltzes. For the dancer this will influence what steps are used and the feel of the dance but there are no longer any hard and fast rules

These steps can be anything you like but are most often a walk or a skip step, certainly for beginners, with a sideways gallop being about the only other step you will need to start with. Others like the polka can be introduced later and are included in the glossary

Glossary of Dance Figures

In & Out – What it says.

Swing …..your Partner. There are many ways to swing but to start with I suggest linking right arms and going around each other, then changing arms. Another version is to do a cross hand hold with your partner but this can get a bit wild and slightly dangerous in confined spaces. For adults the traditional favourite is the pivot swing, taking a ballroom hold and describing a small circle with the two right feet while providing the push with the left.

Here is the second half of the swing

Promenade – Walking or skipping around the circle. For young children just holding hands is fine but the traditional way I to use both hands, right hand holding right and left holding left, so the hands are held across in front of the body. Usually done in an anti-clockwise direction.

Right (& Left) Hand Turn – Give your partner your left hand, as though shaking hands, and walk or skip all the way around until you are back to your place. For the left hand turn change hands and go back the other way.

Two Hand Turn – Can be done two ways. Cross handed as in the text of Sandridge Reel, linking right hands over left or Open Handed so just joining hands with your partner.

Back to Back (or Do-si-do) – Stand facing your partner, then pass by the right shoulder and move to the right behind each other, and then return to your place passing by the left shoulder. You should remain facing forwards throughout the figure; never turn round to face back the way you've come.

Circle Left and Right – Join hands in a circle and do what it says.

Right (& Left) Hand Star – All put your right hands into the middle and join with the person opposite (in olden days it was called Hands Across) and dance around. Change hands and direction for the Left Hand Star.

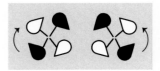

Balance & Swing – The balance is basically just a little step to the right and a step to the left but many people kick their legs across as they do so. Do four of these steps or kicks and then swing your partner round, linking arms is easiest.

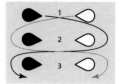

Cross & Weave – First couple cross the set, passing right shoulder, go behind the second couple, cross over again and go behind the third couple

Turn Single – Use 4 small steps to turn around on the spot, bringing your feet together on the 4th. This usually done turning to the right except in much older dances but it does depend on the dance.

Corners Cross – With two couples dancing together you change places with the person diagonally across from you, usually passing right shoulder. Who goes first depends on the dance so check the instructions.

Circular Hey (or Right & Left Through) – All turn to your partner, give them your right hand and change places, turn towards the couple you have been dancing with and give the person facing you your left hand and change places. Now give your partners your right hand and change places one more time and if you turn to face the way you were to start with you should be looking at a new couple. In Mr Cosgill's Delight the dancers do 3 changes, a 4th change (opposite with the left) would bring you back to where you started from.

Giving left hand

In other dances this may start by giving right hands to your opposite but the pattern is the same.

Siding – Walk forwards (and slightly to the left) so you are right shoulder to right shoulder with your partner making eye contact as you do so and then walk backwards to place. Repeat to the left shoulder.

Arming – Link Right Arms at the elbow and dance around your partner once. Change arms and direction for the Arm Left.

NB: this is what I have used for the swing to start with.

Grand Chain – All couples in the circle stand facing their partners. Give right hand to your partner and pass by the right shoulder moving forwards to face the next person, then take left hand and pass by the left shoulder to move to the next, and so on for as many changes are required.

... and left to the next

NB: A Circular Hey and a Grand Chain are the same figure but with different numbers of dancers.

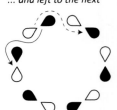

The Steps

Walk	Just what it says but try and do it in time with the music.
Skip	This is just step, hop, step, hop. Most children will do this naturally but adults may have to think about it.
Gallop	This is a sideways step and close.
Heel & Toe	Hopping on one foot touch the heel of the other foot on the floor and then the toe.
Set	Step onto the right foot, close the left then two quick changes of weight so the left foot is free to do the same the other way. A simpler version is just to do the step and close but without changing weight.
Single Step	Just a step and close in the old dances. Can be done forwards backwards or sideways. Nowadays it often means a Skip or a Step Hop.
Double Step	There are many variations of this step but they all start from step, step, step, close as in Right, Left, Right, Together.

The variations of the Double Step include:

Taking the left foot behind when moving sideways as in Left, Right Behind, Left, Together.

Changing the Feet Together for a Hop (ie. R, L, R, hop), this works well in Mr Cosgill's Delight and for chasing around the set in Tars of Victory.

Moving sideways doing Step, Close, Step, Hop is another version of the double step that is called the Polka which you can use instead of the animal impressions in the Ark Lark.

Quick & Easy Dances

1. Circassian Circle

The original dance of this name appeared in England in the mid 19th century as part of a dance revolution that took place after the Napoleonic wars. What we have here is just one figure which used to be called The Big Set and is often used as the last dance at a Barn Dance just so everyone can join in as it really is one of the simplest dances in the book.

> **Formation** – couples in a circle, holding hands. Numbering 1 & 2 (clockwise) or, if you are dancing as boys & girls then the boy would have his partner on his right or the girl has the boy on her left.

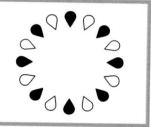

Music – This dance can be danced many different styles of music, pretty much anything with 32 bars. We are going to suggest an exciting set of jigs on **Track 8** (see note on page 24).

Instructions

A1   All dance four steps in towards the middle and back again. Do this again.

A2   All #1s (or girls) dance four steps in clapping hands on the 4th step then coming back to place.

All #2s (or boys) do the same.

B1   Swing your partners. Suggestion - if partners link right arms, go around once, then turn & link left arms (see glossary illustration).

B2   All promenade anti-clockwise two-by-two around the circle. For young dancers it might be simpler for them just to hold hands. The traditional hold is to use both hands, right hand holding right & left holding left so the hands are held across in front of the body.

Dance at a glance

1.   All in & out twice
2.   #1s in, clap & out
3.   #2s the same
4.   Swing
5.   Promenade

2. Sandridge Reel

This dance was created at the Brownie Revels in St Albans in October 2014 when each group of 16 brownies had 30 minutes to do two, or in some cases, three dances. This adaption of the well known Virginia Reel proved one of the most successful and was danced by every group.

Music – This dance fits perfectly to **Track 3** (32 bar polkas)

Formation
– 8 couple longways set
– 8 people in a line all facing their partners across the set

Instructions

A1   Hold hands with the person next to you along the line. Forward for 4 steps & back. Do it again.

A2   All move forward to give your partner your right hand and walk all the way round them. This is called a Right Hand Turn.

Repeat the last move using your left hand & go the other way, called a Left Hand Turn.

B1   Keeping the left hand held, join the right over the top, going the way you first went, for a Two Hand Turn.

Face your partner for a Back to Back (or Do-si-do). To do this stand facing your partner, then pass by the right shoulder and move to the right behind each other, and then return to your place passing by the left shoulder.

B2   Top couple (those nearest the music) gallop down to the other end of the set.

All swing your partners.

Dance at a glance

1. Lines Forward & Back twice
2. Right Hand Turn
3. Left Hand Turn
4. Two Hand Turn
5. Back to Back
6. Top couple gallop down
7. All swing

3. Mixer Promenade

This is a nice simple dance that I learnt from caller Tom Brown. Great at the start of an event as it gives everyone a chance to meet other people. There are many variations of this dance around.

Music – Quicksilver usually play the tunes on **Track 6** for this one (32 bar polkas)

Instructions

A1   Join hands in circles of 4 people and go around to the left, called Circle Left.

Change direction and go the other way, called Circle Right.

A2   All put your right hands into the middle, join with the person opposite and walk around the way you are facing. This is called a Right Hand Star.

Change hands and go the other way. This is called a Left Hand Star.

B1   Face your Partner to Balance & Swing. The balance is basically just a little step to the right and a step to the left (see glossary illustration) but many people kick their legs across as they do so. Do four of these steps or kicks and then swing your partner round, linking arms is easiest.

B2   Hold both hands with your partner (right to right & left to left), say goodbye to the other couple and walk anywhere around the room to find another couple to dance with and do it all again. This is called a Promenade from the French 'to walk'.

Dance at a glance
1.   Circle Left & Right
2.   Right & Left Hand Star
3.   Balance & Swing
4.   Promenade

4. Jumping Johnny

This dance is an adaption of an old dance called Jumping Joan made so it fits the music that is available and is not quite so exhausting.

> **Formation** – A circle with one of each couple (the boys if dancing that way) with their backs to the centre and the other one (the girl) facing them. This forms two concentric circles.

Music – Track 7 (24 bar jigs)

Instructions

A   Back to back with your partner passing right shoulder first.

Back to back passing left shoulder first.

B1   Jump in the air twisting Left & Right, this can be four slow jumps each way or 8 quick ones.

B2   Everyone look diagonally to your right to see the next person around in the other circle. Link Right Arm with them and swing round, then left arm. Now you repeat the whole dance with this new partner.

Dance at a glance

1.   Back to back right & left
2.   Jump & twist
3.   Swing the next

5. Oxo Reel

This dance has been around since the middle of the 20th century and is adapted from various dances collected 50 years before that.

Music – This works best to lively 32 bar reels such as **Track 1**

Instructions

A1 All dance forward for 4 steps and back, the dance a Back to Back, right shoulder, with your partner.

A2 Repeat that but this time do a left shoulder Back to Back.

B1 The 2 couples at each end (couples 1 & 2 and 5 & 6) form circles of 4, while the middle couples make a right hand star. Ends circle left & right while the middles star right and left. Looking down from above this spells OXO, which is the instruction.

B2 The top couple gallop to the bottom of the set, everyone moves up a bit and if there is time you swing your partner.

Note: When you start again you will all be in a different place for the OXO.

Dance at a glance

1. Lines forward & back
2. Back to back right
3. Repeat 1 and 2 with back to back left
4. Oxo
5. Gallop (& swing if there is time)

13

6. Ark Lark

This variation of the older & more famous Pat-a-Cake Polka comes from Alan Simpson one of Quicksilver's regular callers

Music – Track 9 (16 bar polkas)

Formation – Circle but facing your partner

Instructions

A1 (4 bars) All take 2 hands with your partner & with the foot nearest the centre tap your heel & then your toe on the floor twice (you can hop with the other foot at the same time), then gallop 4 steps in that direction.

A2 Do the same with the outside foot (heel & toe, heel & toe) and gallop back.

B1 Clapping; right hand to right hand 3 times; Left to left 3 times; Both 3 times & knees (your own) three times. That is:

Right, right, right, left, left, left, both, both, both & knees, knees, knees

B2 Everyone pretend to be a chicken or whatever animal the caller chooses, a different one each time; eg. ducks, sheep, dinosaurs! The original dance had a polka with your partner at this point (see glossary for polka description).

Dance at a glance
1. Heel & Toe, Gallop In
2. Heel & Toe, Gallop out
3. Clapping
4. Animal Impressions

7. Tars of Victory

The original dance appeared in a collection of dances by Thomas Wilson in 1809. It was then included in Bold Nelson's Praise, a collection put together to celebrate the Battle of Trafalgar. I took the dance and changed the shape of the dance and the last figure creating a very simple dance that has become very popular wherever I teach it.

Formation –
A Square Set – 4 couples standing with their partner next to them in a circle. When you let go hands with the other couples you should find that each couple is on one side of a square

Music – Track 6 or Track 8

Instructions

A1   The person on the right of the 1st couple sets off to the right and, followed by their partner, goes all the way around the outside (anti-clockwise).

A2   Turn round and go the other way (clockwise) so this time the other person does the chasing.

B1   Everyone join two hands in a promenade hold (right to right and left to left) and dances anti-clockwise around the set.

B2   All swing your partners.

Repeat with 2nd couple, 3rd couple & 4th couple. Then if using Track 6 try 1st & 3rd together then 2nd & 4th, if using Track 8 give everyone a second go and the very last time through have everyone chasing at once.

I sometimes change the promenade figure for some back to backs.

Dance at a glance

1.   Chase anti-clockwise
2.   Chase clockwise
3.   Promenade
4.   Swing

Quite Simple Dances

8. Hop Pickers Picnic

This is an adaptation of an 18th century dance called the Hop Pickers feast. It can be danced as you have danced all the other dances, or use it as an opportunity to add some steps and styles from the past.

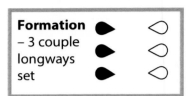

Formation – 3 couple longways set

Formation – 3 couple longways set

Music - For real style the best track on the is **Track 6** (32 bar polkas) but for a more lively version try **Track 1** (32 bar reels)

Instructions

A1   First couple turn to face the 2nd lady and set right & left to her, twice, then join hands in a circle of three and circle left until back to place.

To set right; take small step to the right, bring the left foot to meet and step back onto the right. This involves 3 quick changes of weight and takes a bit of practice to look really elegant. Reverse the order of the feet for set left.

A2   First couple do the same with the second man.

B1   First couple cross the set, passing right shoulder, go behind the second couple, cross over again and go behind the third couple (see Cross and Weave in the glossary), and everyone turn single (that is turn around in the spot) in your new place.

The stepping for this would have been "hop, step, close, step" with the body nice and upright, but this would often have been simplified to a polka or double step.

B2   All join hands in a circle of 6 and slip step (step close) around to the left for 8 and back to the right.

Dance at a glance

1. First couple set to 2nd lady
2. Circle 3
3. Repeat to 2nd Man
4. Cross & Weave to the bottom
5. All turn single
6. All circle left & right

16

9. Mr Cosgill's Delight

This dance was in the New Country Dancing Master (3rd book) published by Walsh in 1728 and the music was from a piece by Corelli written in 1685.

Music – Track 5 is Quicksilver's version of the original tune (16 bar schottische); a type of hornpipe

Formation – Originally a longways set for "as many as will" but it is simpler to learn it as a circular dance in what is called Sicilian Circle. This is formed by small sets of two couples facing each other around the large circle. Where a boy & girl are dancing together then the boy should be on the left of the couple; otherwise make it 1's on the left 2's on the right

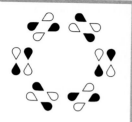

Steps – I recommend the variation of the double-step described on page 8.

Instructions

A1 Right hand star in your fours.

A2 Left hand star back again.

B1 Boys (or #1s) change places (2 steps), Girls (or #2s) change places.

All turn left and walk four steps around the small circle back to place.

B2 All turn to your partner, give them your right hand and change places, turn towards the couple you have been dancing with and give the person facing you your left hand and change places. Now give your partners your right hand and change places one more time and if you turn to face the way you were to start with you should be looking at a new couple.

(This is called a circular hey or Right & Left through.)

A simpler B2: Join hands with your partner, walk forwards to meet the other couple, back away and walk forwards , passing the other couple by the right shoulder to change places – don't turn around.

Dance at a glance

1. Right & Left hand stars
2. corners cross & walk back
3. 3 changes of a circular hey OR forward, back & pass on

Giving left hand

10. The Haystack

I think this dance started when I realised that Haymakers jig might be a bit complex for a group of Brownies with a Harvest themed event but little is left of the original.

Music – **Track 1** (32 bar reels) or **Track 8** (32 bar jigs) but you might not want to dance it nine times through

Formation – designed as a square set, that is four couples standing next to each other in a circle, but there seems to be no reason why it cannot be 3, 4, 5 or even 6 couples in a small circle (though 6 would have to be quick). If a boy & girl are dancing together the boy should be on the left

Instructions

A1   Join hands and go four steps in & four steps out, twice.

A2   Turn away from your partner and Balance & Swing the one you meet – this is your corner.

B1   Turn back to your partner & balance a swing with them.

B2   Grand Chain - Making sure you are back in your place before you start, give your partner your right hand, pass them by, give left hands to the next and so on, all the way around the set, meeting your partner half way round and carrying on until you get back to place.

Dance at a glance

1. In & Out twice
2. Balance & swing corner
3. Balance & swing partner
4. Grand chain

... and left to the next

18

11. Barley Water

The dance called Juice of Barley from the 17th century can be a bit of a challenge but it is a great tune and Quicksilver included a very short version of the tune on the CD. So here is a shortened dance which starts off the same but then gets a bit simpler.

Music – Track 7

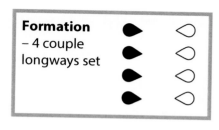

Formation
– 4 couple longways set

Instructions

A   All back to back with your partners, passing right shoulder.

All two hand turn with your partners, travelling clockwise.

B1   1st couple weave to the bottom going between the 2nd, outside the 3rd and between the 4th. Don't confuse this with Cross and Weave - just weave down your own line, with no crossing over.

All clap & turn two hands again.

B2   Join right hands in fours and do a right and left hand star. These fours will be the 2nd & 3rd couples who have moved up to the top and the 4th & 1st couples, who are now at the bottom.

Dance at a glance
1. Back to back, right shoulders
2. Two hand turn, clockwise
3. Weave
4. All clap & two hand turn
5. Right & left hand star in fours

Rather Older Dances

12. Clog Brawle

This is very old dance, even when it was first published in 1589 and does not fit the pattern of even phrase lengths, nor does it require a partner. It uses double steps which in their simplest form are Left, Right, Left & Close or Right, Left, Right & Close. The stamps at the end imitate the sound of clogs which are shoes with wooden soles.

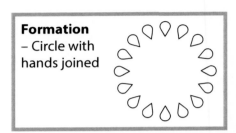

Formation
– Circle with hands joined

Music – this has its own tune on **Track 10**

A   Double step left, Double step right; do that again.

For younger dancers it is sometimes easier to go 7 steps to the left, stop and come back.

B   Facing the middle all Step Left & Close, Step Right & Close (these are single steps), 3 stamps on the right foot; repeat.

Dance at a glance
1. Double left & right twice
2. Single left & right
3. 3 stamps
4. Repeat 2 & 3

13. Washerwoman's Brawle

This dance comes from the same collection as the Clog Brawle and has many similarities but you do need partners.

Formation – Partners in a circle with hands joined. Number 1 & 2 going anti-clockwise around the set

Formation
– Partners in a circle with hands joined. Number 1 & 2 anti-clockwise around the set

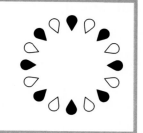

Music – this has its own tune on **Track 10**

A   Double step left, Double step right; twice.

For younger dancers it is sometimes easier to go 7 steps to the left, stop and come back for 7.

B1   Face Partners, #1s take a (single) step to the left & step to the right wagging a finger at your partner while #2s stand still with arms folded or hands on hips (we want attitude!)

B2   Repeat with #2s stepping and #1s with attitude.

C   All face the middle; 2 side steps left while clapping twice, 2 side steps right with no claps, 2 left with claps and 4 jumps left, right, left, right (these can be called capers or spring points depending on your dance background).

Dance at a glance

1.   Double left & right twice
2.   #1s single left, right, wag finger
3.   #2s single left, right, wag finger
4.   Side step left with claps
5.   Side step right, no claps
6.   Side step left with claps
7.   Four jumps

14. Sellingers Round

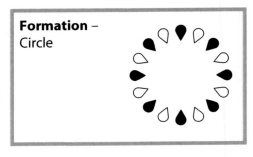

Formation –
Circle

This very popular dance was probably introduced to the court of Elizabeth the First as it is mentioned in plays long before it was published in 1651. The sequence of a Figure followed by a Chorus became very common. It is around this time that country dancing as we now know it first appeared. In keeping with dancing of the 17th century I have suggested that everything starts on the left foot.

For teaching purposes I often call the figures verses. Those who have learnt it elsewhere may prefer to use the right foot first. This only really matters in the Chorus figure where the Single Left & Right becomes Set Right & Left.

Music – Track 2

Verse 1	Circle Left & Right
Chorus	Single (step & close) moving Left and Single Right moving in
	Double Back (right left right and close)
	Facing Partner Single Left and Single Right
	Turn around to left using double step
	Repeat all of that
Verse 2	Siding with Partner (a double step shoulder to shoulder)
	Make sure you have real eye contact
	The same the other side
Chorus	
Verse 3	Arm Right with Partner
	Arm Left with Partner
Chorus	
Verse 4	is the same as Verse 1
Chorus	

Dance at a glance

1. Circle Left & Right
2. Chorus
3. Siding
4. Chorus
5. Arming
6. Chorus
7. Repeat #1
8. Chorus

15. Farandole

Formation – ♡♡♡♡♡♡♡
Everyone in a
line with hands held low and loose

This dance often with different names is very, very old. There are all sorts of pictures showing people dancing these sorts of things and there is a very famous one from 15th century Sienna in Italy. The first 3 figures definitely qualify as Quick & Easy and can be used on their own. The other figures can be added in later.

Formation -

Music – this dance is not phrased so anything works. If you want to keep it short and lively then use **Track 12**. If you want to try all the figures then **Track 4** may be better.

The Circle	Just lead round in a circle.
The Meander	Now lead the line in Zig Zags.
The Snail	Get the line going clockwise in a circle then spiral in getting tighter and tighter. When completely wrapped up can reverse between the lines or dive out through arches between dancers.
Arches	Leader turns back and goes through arch made by 2&3 then 3&4 etc everyone following.
Thread the Needle	Dancers 1&2 make an arch over 3, leaving them as new leader and arching over everyone go to the back of the line.
The Hey	Divide the line in two and then approach leaders give right hands to each other, left to the next and so on down the line, reforming lines as everyone emerges.
Over the Top	Like Thread the Needle but everyone joins the arches Through the Tunnel In pairs following previous figure now first couple dive underneath arch made by second couple.

This book was designed to go with the CD Maypole Madness but some of you will be using it as a supplement to The Maypole Manual and the CD that goes with it. The tracks are in a slightly different order on the two CDs so here is the key to which tracks we suggest.

If you suddenly find you have real live musicians then I have given the information they will need. The numbers mean how many bars; J = jig, R = reel, P = polka, H = hornpipe (or Sch = Schottische). *Specific tunes exist for dances 7, 8, 9, 11, 12, 13 & 14. If you want the music contact me and I'll email it.

	Dance Title	Maypole Madness Track	Maypole Manual Track	Music Needed
1	Circassian Circle	8	3	32 J or R
2	Sandridge Reel	3	2	32 P
3	Mixer Promenade	6	6	32 P
4	Jumping Johnny	7	5	24 J
5	Oxo Reel	1	1 or 4	32 R
6	Ark Lark	9	10	16 P
7	Tars of Victory	6 or 8	6 or 3	32 P or J*
8	Hop Pickers Picnic	6 or 1	6 or 1	32 P or R*
9	Mr Cosgill's Delight	5	8	16 H (Sch)*
10	The Haystack	1 or 8	1, 3, or 9	32 R or J
11	Barley Water	7	5	24 J*
12	Clog Brawle	10	11	Own tune
13	Washerwoman's Brawle	11	12	Own tune
14	Sellinger's Round	2	13	24 J*
15	Farandole	12	14 or 7	any

Mike Ruff

Mike Ruff started dancing in his teens and called his first dance within a year or two. His first regular calling was when he moved to London. Since then he has danced, called, taught and performed at all sorts of events even as far away as Germany and Australia. Some have been small workshops or Brownie packs, others have been festival ceilidhs or corporate events for hundreds of dancers.

Mike is always interested in exploring the historical background and contemporary possibilities to do with country dancing. Recently he has started training a new generation of teachers and has been involved in choreography for theatre shows. His talks on the history and development of English Country Dance and related topics are finding new audiences for this aspect of our cultural heritage.

His work in schools through Tradamis gave him an insight into the challenges of introducing dance and the need for clear, user friendly resources. Mike has co-authored The Maypole Manual and wrote Morris! Hey! He is currently working on Dancing Through History

Quicksilver

Mike Ruff set up Quicksilver almost 30 years ago after the demise of a couple of other bands. Always based around the best musicians available but with a real feel for the dancing. The core line-up of Mike (accordion), Chris Haigh (fiddle) and Bernard O'Neill (bass) lasted until 2014. Many other musicians have been involved and Graeme Taylor (guitar) and Andy Dewar (drums) have been regulars whenever possible. Tom Fairbairn has now replaced Bernard on bass and keyboards allowing Mike to take up more of the calling.

Quicksilver have played many events large and small and travelled throughout England (and even into Scotland) playing at weddings, corporate events, festivals and every other sort of celebration you can imagine; and yes they even do Bar Mitzvahs. Definitely more than just a band so find out more and see them in action at www.quicksilverbarndance.com

Other Publications by Mike Ruff

The Maypole Manual
(with Jenny Read)

This comprehensive guide to Maypole Dancing has the standard traditional dances as collated by John Ruskin, contemporary dances suitable for today's dancers and some dances from previous centuries before ribbons got added to Maypoles. Something for everyone with the dances graded in order of difficulty. Full colour illustrations and simple diagrams to go with a clear text. Just add a Maypole.

£30 + p&p from www.mikesmaypole.co.uk and www.mikeruffmusic.co.uk

Morris! Hey!

"The next step in Morris Dance Teaching". A double DVD plus book & CD giving detailed instructions on 6 dances from the main Morris traditions; Cotswold, North-West, Border and Molly featuring Fool's Gambit Morris. The dances are broken down into easy to follow instructions and the book backs this up with diagrams, detailed instructions and more hints. Starter packs of sticks, bells and hankies in club and class size will also be available.

Amazing introductory price £40 + p&p from www.themorrisshop.com